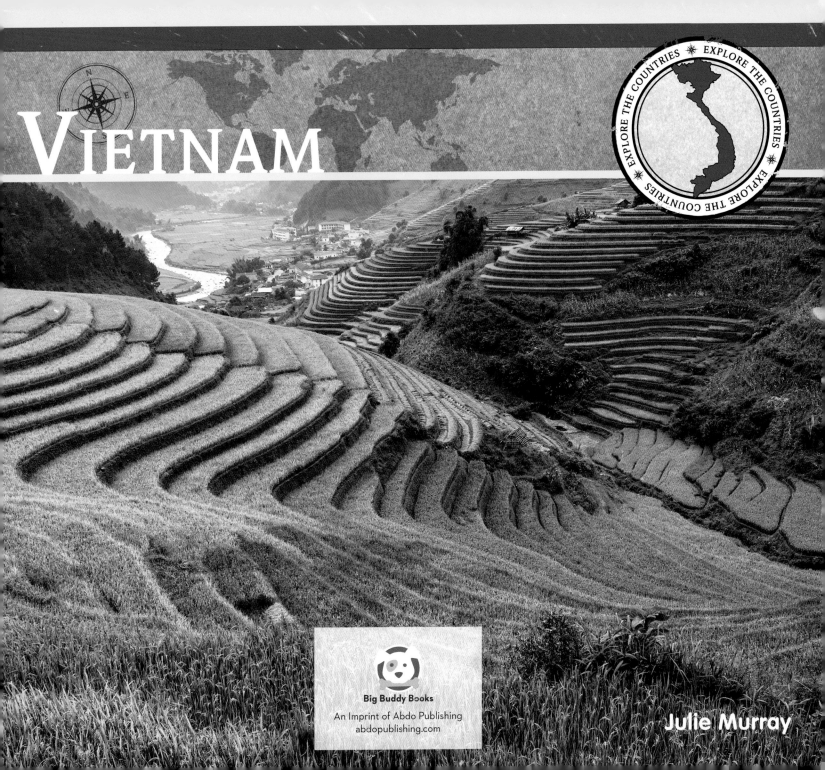

VIETNAM

EXPLORE THE COUNTRIES

Big Buddy Books
An Imprint of Abdo Publishing
abdopublishing.com

Julie Murray

abdopublishing.com

Published by Abdo Publishing, a division of ABDO, PO Box 398166, Minneapolis, Minnesota 55439.
Copyright © 2018 by Abdo Consulting Group, Inc. International copyrights reserved in all countries. No part
of this book may be reproduced in any form without written permission from the publisher. Big Buddy Books™
is a trademark and logo of Abdo Publishing.

Printed in the United States of America, North Mankato, Minnesota.
052017
092017

Cover Photo: ©iStockphoto.com.
Interior Photos: ASSOCIATED PRESS (p. 33); Dave Bedrosian/Geisler-Fotopress/picture-alliance/dpa/AP
    Images (p. 33); JORDI CAMÍ/Alamy Stock Photo (p. 29); CPA Media - Pictures from History/Granger,
    NYC — All rights reserved. (pp. 13, 16); DeA Picture Library/Granger, NYC — All rights reserved.
    (p. 13); dpa picture alliance archive/Alamy Stock Photo (p. 19); Hemis/Alamy Stock Photo (p. 5); Bob
    Henry/Alamy Stock Photo (p. 35); imageBROKER / Alamy Stock Photo (p. 31); ©iStockphoto.com
    (pp. 9, 11, 21, 23, 27, 29, 34, 35, 38); Hakbong Kwon/Alamy Stock Photo (p. 35); Mauro Ladu/Alamy
    Stock Photo (p. 11); Pete Niesen/Alamy Stock Photo (p. 17); Tim Plowden/Alamy Stock Photo (p. 23);
    Shutterstock.com (pp. 25, 37); SPUTNIK/Alamy Stock Photo (p. 31); Robert Wyatt/Alamy Stock Photo
    (p. 15); Xinhua/Alamy Stock Photo (p. 19).

Coordinating Series Editor: Tamara L. Britton
Editor: Katie Lajiness
Graphic Design: Taylor Higgins, Keely McKernan

Country population and area figures taken from the CIA World Factbook.

Publisher's Cataloging-in-Publication Data

Names: Murray, Julie, 1969- , author.
Title: Vietnam / by Julie Murray.
Description: Minneapolis, MN : Abdo Publishing, 2018. | Series: Explore the
    countries | Includes bibliographical references and index.
Identifiers: LCCN 2016962356 | ISBN 9781532110559 (lib. bdg.) |
    ISBN 9781680788402 (ebook)
Subjects: LCSH: Vietnam--Juvenile literature.
Classification: DDC 959.7--dc23
LC record available at http://lccn.loc.gov/2016962356

Vietnam

Contents

Around the World 4

Passport to Vietnam. 6

Important Cities 8

Vietnam in History. 12

Timeline 16

An Important Symbol 18

Across the Land 20

Earning a Living 24

Life in Vietnam. 26

Famous Faces 30

Tour Book 34

A Great Country 36

Vietnam Up Close 38

Important Words 39

Websites. 39

Index 40

AROUND THE WORLD

Our world has many countries. Each country has beautiful land. It has its own rich history. And, the people have their own languages and ways of life.

Vietnam is a country in Asia. What do you know about Vietnam? Let's learn more about this place and its story!

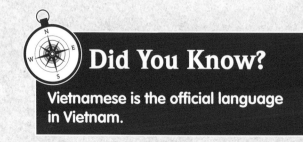

Did You Know?

Vietnamese is the official language in Vietnam.

4

The Ho Chi Minh City Hall was completed in 1908. Built by the French, the building was made to look like a Paris hotel.

CHỦ TỊCH HỒ CHÍ MINH
(1890 - 1969)

SAY IT

Vietnam
vee-EHT-nahm

PASSPORT TO VIETNAM

Vietnam is a country in Southeast Asia. The country shares a border with China to the north. Vietnam borders Cambodia and Laos to the west. The Gulf of Thailand is to the southwest. The South China Sea is to the east.

The country's total area is 127,881 square miles (331,210 sq km). More than 95 million people live there.

WHERE IN THE WORLD?

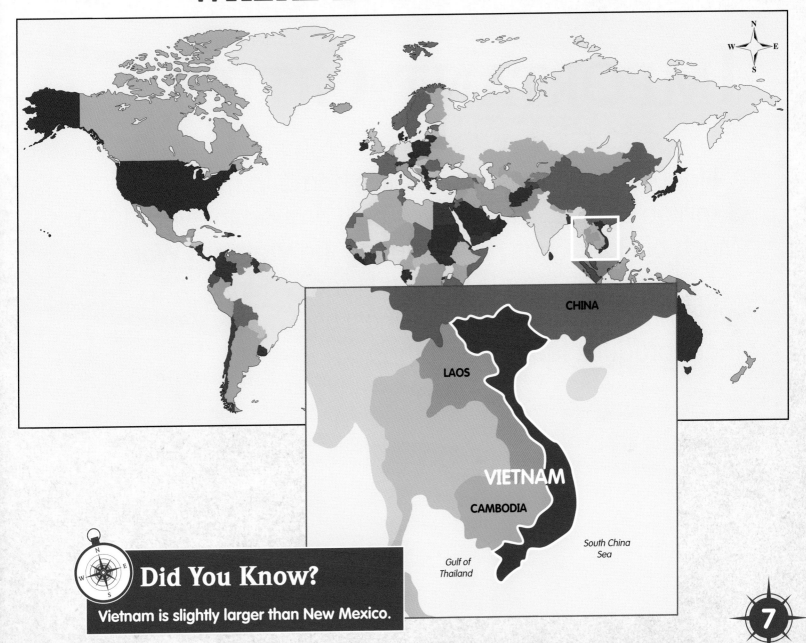

Did You Know?

Vietnam is slightly larger than New Mexico.

CHINA

LAOS

VIETNAM

CAMBODIA

South China
Sea

Gulf of
Thailand

IMPORTANT CITIES

Hanoi is Vietnam's **capital**. It is home to more than 3 million people. The city was built around the year 1000. Much of Hanoi was ruined during the **Vietnam War**.

Today, many people work in Hanoi's banks, government, and private businesses. Factory workers there produce food and clothes.

SAY IT

Hanoi
ha-NOY

VIETNAM

★ Hanoi

● Ho Chi Minh City
● Can Tho

The Temple of Literature was built in 1070. It is Vietnam's first university.

Ho Chi Minh City is Vietnam's largest city. It is home to more than 7 million people. Today, the city has many markets with people selling food and other goods. Factory workers make bicycles, clothes, machinery, rubber, and soap.

Can Tho is in southern Vietnam. More than 1 million people live there. Originally part of Cambodia, the city became part of Vietnam during the 1700s. Can Tho is known for its large inland port. People there make bricks, fish sauce, ice, and plastics.

In 1976, the city of Saigon was renamed Ho Chi Minh City.

The Can Tho floating market features many boats filled with goods. People can buy fruits, vegetables, and other products.

Vietnam in History

People have lived in Vietnam since 3000 BC. Tribes from southern China traveled to the Red River Delta area. There, they met many Indonesian people. These two groups became the Vietnamese people.

Over the years, many groups came to Vietnam and tried to take over. During the 1800s, the French controlled Vietnam. The people were forced to learn about European **culture**.

During the mid-1800s, French explorers drew pictures of their adventures in Vietnam. These drawings were later printed in books.

After **World War I**, Ho Chi Minh became a voice for Vietnam's independence. In 1941, he created a group called the Viet Minh. After **World War II**, it took over Hanoi. Then the Viet Minh formed a **Communist** state. In 1954, Vietnam split. The northern part was Communist. The southern part was not.

The **Vietnam War** was fought from 1954 to 1975. After the war, Communists took over South Vietnam. Life was hard for the Vietnamese people. They suffered as the country joined together after the war. Then the country began to create more jobs. And, people were able to build better lives.

The Vietnam War Memorial was built in 1993.
It honors those who died during the war.

TIMELINE

207 BC

The kingdom of Nam-Viet was formed. Today, this land is in northern Vietnam and southern China.

AD **1802**

Ruler Nguyen Anh united the areas and formed a country. He called it Vietnam.

1930

Ho Chi Minh created the Indochinese **Communist** Party.

1940

During **World War II**, Japan took over Vietnam.

1976

North and South Vietnam were united under **Communist** leadership.

2012

Vietnam passed Brazil to become the world's largest coffee supplier.

An Important Symbol

Vietnam's flag is red with a gold star. This flag was adopted in 1945.

Vietnam is a **Communist** country. The president is the head of state. The president appoints the prime minister, who is the head of government.

The country has 58 provinces. This is a large section within a country, like a state.

The flag's five-pointed star stands for the five groups of workers in Vietnam.

SAY IT

Tran Dai Quang
CHUHNG DAY KWAWNG

Tran Dai Quang became Vietnam's president in 2016.

SAY IT

Nguyen Tan Dung
WIHN TUHNG YOONG

Nguyen Tan Dung is the prime minister. He was first elected in 2006 and re-elected in 2011.

ACROSS THE LAND

Vietnam has mountains, lowlands, jungles, and forests. The country's highest point is Fan Si Pan. It stands 10,315 feet (3,144 m) high.

Vietnam has two **monsoon** seasons. The winter winds bring dry, cold air. The summer winds bring hot, wet weather and heavy rains.

Did You Know?

In Hanoi, the average temperature is 63°F (17°C) in January. In June, it is 85°F (29°C).

The Fan Si Pan mountain range runs about 19 miles (31 km) long between the Red and Black Rivers.

Nearly half of Vietnam is covered by forest. Beech, chestnut, ebony, and pine trees grow throughout the country. Bamboo plants grow in many places.

Vietnam is home to different kinds of animals. Black bears, elephants, tigers, and wild pigs live in the forests. Crocodiles are found along riverbanks and in lakes.

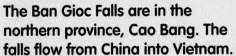

The Ban Gioc Falls are in the northern province, Cao Bang. The falls flow from China into Vietnam.

The Son Tra Nature Center in Da Nang is home to 200 red-shanked douc monkeys. Few of these monkeys remain in the wild.

Earning a Living

Most of Vietnam's workers are farmers. Rice is the country's main crop. Other crops include coffee, corn, peanuts, and sweet potatoes.

Fishing is another important job in Vietnam. Workers raise or catch shrimp, catfish, and tuna.

People in Vietnam also produce goods. Factory workers make phones, clothes, food, and steel.

Workers collect salt from sun-dried, shallow pools of sea water. They carry the salt to the factory in baskets.

LIFE IN VIETNAM

Vietnam has a rich **cultural** history. The country has great art and food. The Vietnamese are known for their baskets, fine needlework, and paintings.

Like most Asian countries, Vietnamese meals are served with rice. Noodle soups with chicken or beef broth are also popular.

In Hoi An, silk lanterns are a popular item. They are made from silk, bamboo, and wood.

27

Many people in Vietnam enjoy watching and playing sports. Badminton, cycling, and soccer are common sports. Karate and tae kwon do are practiced throughout the country.

In Vietnam, **Buddhism** is the major religion. But, many people follow other Vietnamese religions or **Christianity**.

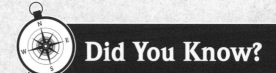

Did You Know?

In Vietnam, children must attend school from ages 6 through 11. Most Vietnamese can read and write.

People visit Buddhist temples to feel at peace.

Tae kwon do is a popular sport in Vietnam. It is the martial art of kicking and punching.

29

FAMOUS FACES

Many famous people are from Vietnam. Ho Chi Minh was a **Communist** leader. He was born on May 19, 1890, in Hoang Tru, Vietnam.

Minh was president of North Vietnam from 1945 to 1969. In 1969, he died while the **Vietnam War** was being fought. Minh's legacy lives on in Vietnam. The country's largest city is named after him.

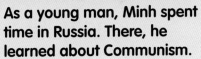

As a young man, Minh spent time in Russia. There, he learned about Communism.

Ho Chi Minh Mausoleum is in Hanoi. It is a memorial for the Vietnamese leader. His body is kept in a special coffin.

Xuan Vinh Hoang was born on October 6, 1974, in Hanoi, Vietnam. He is an Olympic pistol shooter. At the 2012 Olympics in London, England, Hoang did not earn a medal. But he did not give up on his dreams. At the 2016 Olympics in Rio de Janeiro, Brazil, Hoang won Vietnam's first gold medal!

Michelle Phan was born in Boston, Massachusetts, on April 11, 1987. Her parents moved from Vietnam before she was born. At 19, Phan made her first makeup video and posted it online. She used the success from her YouTube videos to start her own company.

SAY IT

Xuan Vinh Hoang
SUHNG VIHN HWAHNG

Hoang first learned how to shoot in Vietnam's military.

Phan uses her fame to help others. She wants to teach women how to start their own businesses.

TOUR BOOK

   Imagine traveling to Vietnam! Here are some places you could go and things you could do.

 **Taste**

Pho is Vietnam's national dish. This noodle soup is a popular street food.

 Celebrate

Tet is the Vietnamese New Year. It is the most important holiday of the year. Honor Tet by eating good food and spending time with family.

 # Learn

The Vietnam Military History Museum is in Hanoi. It is one of seven national museums in Vietnam. Outside the building, visitors can see tanks used during the war.

 # Shop

The Ben Thanh Market is in Ho Chi Minh City. It is one of the oldest markets in the city. People there sell clothes, crafts, and foods.

 # Relax

Many people travel through the streets on cyclos. This three-wheel bicycle taxi is used in busy cities.

A GREAT COUNTRY

The story of Vietnam is important to our world. Vietnam is a land of tasty foods and beautiful views. It is a country of strong people who have a rich history.

The people and places that make up Vietnam offer something special. They help make the world a more beautiful, interesting place.

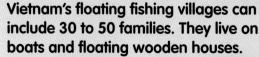

Vietnam's floating fishing villages can include 30 to 50 families. They live on boats and floating wooden houses.

VIETNAM UP CLOSE

Official Name: Socialist Republic of Vietnam

Flag:

Population (rank): 95,261,021
(July 2016 est.)
(15th most-populated country)

Total Area (rank): 127,881 square miles
(66th largest country)

Capital: Hanoi

Official Language: Vietnamese

Currency: Vietnamese dong

Form of Government: Communist state

National Anthem: "Tien Quan Ca"
("The Song of the Marching Troops")

IMPORTANT WORDS

Buddhism (BOO-dih-zuhm) a religion based on the teachings of Buddha.

capital a city where government leaders meet.

Christianity (KRIHS-chee-A-nuh-tee) a religion that follows the teachings of Jesus Christ.

Communist (KAHM-yuh-nihst) of or relating to a form of government in which all or most land and goods are owned by the state. They are then divided among the people based on need.

culture (KUHL-chuhr) the arts, beliefs, and ways of life of a group of people.

monsoon a seasonal wind in southern Asia that sometimes brings heavy rain.

Vietnam War a war that took place between South Vietnam and North Vietnam from 1957 to 1975. The United States was involved in this war for many years.

World War I a war fought in Europe from 1914 to 1918.

World War II a war fought in Europe, Asia, and Africa from 1939 to 1945.

WEBSITES

To learn more about Explore the Countries, visit **abdobooklinks.com**. These links are routinely monitored and updated to provide the most current information available.

INDEX

animals **13, 22, 23**

Asia **4, 6, 26**

Ben Thanh Market **35**

Brazil **17, 32**

businesses **8, 10, 11, 17, 24, 25, 32, 33, 35**

Cambodia **6, 7, 10**

Can Tho **9, 10, 11**

China **6, 7, 12, 16, 23**

England **32**

food **8, 10, 11, 17, 24, 26, 34, 36**

France **5, 7, 12, 13**

government **8, 14, 16, 17, 18, 19, 30, 38**

Gulf of Thailand **6, 7**

Hanoi **5, 8, 9, 14, 20, 31, 32, 35, 38**

Hoi An **27**

Ho Chi Minh City **10, 11, 35**

Ho Chi Minh City Hall **5**

language **4, 38**

Laos **6, 7**

Massachusetts **32**

Minh, Ho Chi **14, 16, 30, 31**

New Mexico **7**

Nguyen, Anh **16**

Nguyen, Tan Dung **19**

Phan, Michelle **32, 33**

plants **22**

population **6, 8, 10, 38**

Red River Delta **12**

religion **28, 29**

Saigon **11**

size **6, 38**

South China Sea **6, 7**

sports **28, 29, 32, 33**

Temple of Literature, **9**

Tran, Dai Quang **19**

Vietnam Military History Museum **35**

Vietnam War **8, 14, 15, 30**

Vietnam War Memorial **15**

weather **20**

Xuan, Vinh Hoang **32, 33**